News From Abroad and the Foreign Policy Public

by W. Phillips Davison, Donald R. Shanor and Frederick T. C. Yu

CONTENTS

1 The News Media, Foreign Policy, and the Public... 3
2 What Is International News? 5
3 How Foreign News Is Covered................... 16
4 Delivering the News........................... 33
5 Audiences for International News................ 43
6 Conclusion: The Media and the 'Active' Public..... 58

Talking It Over 62

HEADLINE Series 250, August 1980 $2.00

Cover design: Design Works

The Authors

W. PHILLIPS DAVISON is professor of Journalism and Sociology at Columbia University, where he also directs the Center for Advanced Study of Communication and Public Affairs at the Graduate School of Journalism. He is a former editor of the *Public Opinion Quarterly*.

DONALD R. SHANOR is professor of Journalism at Columbia University. He was a United Press International correspondent for ten years and subsequently covered Eastern Europe, Germany and the Middle East for the *Chicago Daily News*.

FREDERICK T.C. YU is professor of Journalism at Columbia University. An authority on the mass media in the People's Republic of China, he visited that country early in 1980 at the invitation of the official New China News Agency.

The Foreign Policy Association

The Foreign Policy Association is a private, nonprofit, nonpartisan educational organization. Its purpose is to stimulate wider interest and more effective participation in, and greater understanding of, world affairs among American citizens. Among its activities is the continuous publication, dating from 1935, of the HEADLINE Series pamphlets. The authors of these pamphlets are responsible for factual accuracy and for the views expressed. FPA itself takes no position on issues of United States foreign policy.

Editorial Advisory Committee
Hans J. Morgenthau,* *chairman*

W. Phillips Davison
John Lewis Gaddis
Keith Goldhammer
Antonie T. Knoppers

William H. McNeill
Edwin Newman
Stanley E. Spangler
Richard H. Ullman

*Died July 19, 1980.

The HEADLINE Series (ISSN 0017-8780) is published February, April, August, October and December by the Foreign Policy Association, Inc., 205 Lexington Ave., New York, N.Y. 10016. Chairman, Carter L. Burgess; Editor, Wallace Irwin, Jr.; Associate Editor, Gwen Crowe. Subscription rates, $8.00 for 5 issues; $15.00 for 10 issues; $21.00 for 15 issues. Single copy price $2.00. Discount 25% on 10 to 99 copies; 30% on 100 to 499; 35% on 500 to 999; 40% on 1,000 or more. Payment must accompany order for $5 or less. Second-class postage paid at New York, N.Y. Copyright 1980 by Foreign Policy Association, Inc. Composed and printed at Science Press, Ephrata, Pa.

Library of Congress Catalog No. 80-68024
ISBN 0-87124-063-7

1
The News Media, Foreign Policy, and the Public

How much do Americans learn about world affairs from the news media? Can they become well enough informed to exert a constructive influence on American foreign policy?

These and related questions have been debated for many years. Some democratic theorists have argued that foreign policy, like domestic policy, should be an expression of the popular will. In their view, a citizenry that is well informed about international affairs is essential. Others, while agreeing that popular control of foreign policy is a desirable ideal, have maintained that the complexities of international relations are too great for the average citizen to grasp; foreign affairs are best left to those who are professionally trained to handle them. The late Walter Lippmann characterized the ideal of an informed citizenry as "bad only in the sense that it is bad for a fat man to try to be a ballet dancer." It was unrealistic, he felt, to expect members of the public to take the time and trouble to acquire the necessary information.

Whatever their positions in this debate, the parties to it have usually agreed that the quality of international coverage by the news media is one of the major factors determining the role that the public can and should play in the conduct of foreign relations. Whether the press does a good job or a poor one, it is the principal channel through which the public is informed. The historian Ralph B. Levering, in a recent analysis of the part popular sentiment has played in modern American foreign policy, concludes: "Despite their weaknesses, the media have been the most important link between officials and the public in the formulation of American foreign policy."

In the following pages we will describe the processes through which the mass media provide world affairs information to the public and the ways various groups in the population make use of the information that is made available to them. Specifically, we will focus on four subjects:

1. The nature of "foreign news" and news in general, and how the American definition of news differs from that in other parts of the world.

2. How foreign news is gathered by American news organizations.

3. The winnowing or selective process by which some information about world affairs is finally published or broadcast, while other information is discarded.

4. The extent to which members of the public choose to expose themselves to sources of information about international developments, and how much they learn from these sources.

While we hope that this discussion will contribute to a better understanding of the role of the public in the conduct of American foreign policy, our principal aim is to provide a background against which news and other information about world affairs will become more meaningful. Just as appreciation of a work of art may be heightened if one is acquainted with the circumstances under which it was produced, news from and about foreign countries may be more informative if the consumer is aware of the processes through which it reaches the public. If this essay succeeds in helping the reader to gain more knowledge and enjoyment from the evening news broadcast or the daily newspaper, it will have achieved its purpose.

2
What Is International News?

International news is not easy to define, since there is ample disagreement among both journalists and scholars as to what news is. A former assistant managing editor of *The Washington Post*, Ben Bagdikian, now professor of journalism at the University of California, notes that it is possible to irritate most journalists merely by asking for a definition of news. Though they spend their lives producing it, Bagdikian observes, few reporters can put into words what it is that makes one event newsworthy while another is not. It's like asking a poet for a definition of poetry.

Numerous scholars have analyzed the contents of newspapers and news broadcasts to determine what characteristics of events or developments cause them to be included. Different researchers have reached slightly different conclusions, but most of them agree that an event or development is most likely to be reported in the news media if it—

Has occurred recently;

Concerns a large nation or a well-known individual or group;

Involves conflict—ranging from a difference of opinion to actual fighting;

Is psychologically "close" to people in the audience, or affects substantial numbers of them;

Conforms to prevailing ideas about what the world is like and is not too difficult to understand;

Is part of a continuing story of current interest.

An event that shares several of these characteristics is almost sure to be reported. A hotly fought election in a major European country, for example, involves conflict, concerns an important nation, and is easy to understand. Furthermore, many Americans have family ties in Europe or feel fairly close to one or more European countries.

But if the election is in a small country, perhaps in Africa or Asia, if the issues are difficult to understand, and the country is not already involved in a continuing news story, then it is likely to go unreported.

An event can lack some of the qualities that make for newsworthiness, but if it is very high in other qualities, then it probably will be reported anyway. Thus, the crash of a small airplane in a distant part of the world will be reported if a prominent American is among the victims. And when a small oil-exporting country raises prices on petroleum, this will make headlines because so many people are affected by it.

Sociologist Herbert J. Gans reports that some years ago journalists at an American television network, tongue in cheek, constructed a formula showing that the newsworthiness of an airplane disaster depended not only on the number of people killed but on the country they came from: 100 Czechs were equal to 43 Frenchmen, and so on. Similar examples of wry humor by European journalists have confirmed that "psychological closeness" is an important quality of news in other countries besides the United States.

Practices governing the selection of items for inclusion in the news media of the Western world evolved over several centuries. Many of the earliest newspapers—which began to appear in Europe with the spread of literacy and the printing press in the 16th and 17th centuries—dealt largely with gossip about the royal court, reports of distant battles and information about crops. These were appropriate subjects for inclusion in these papers, since their readers consisted of a small group of persons, most of whom were involved in politics, commerce, or both. It was important to know who was gaining favor with the king or queen, and who was losing favor. News about agriculture and war affected the plans of merchants and moneylenders. A prince who was always losing battles was not a good credit risk, and, as was pointed out by

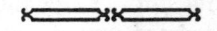

How national affinities influence news play: In November 1979, *The New York Times* reported a Pakistani air disaster, in which 156 people died, on page 11 under a one-column headline. Five months later a British air disaster of comparable size rated a two-column headline on page 1, plus a three-column photograph on page 3.

NO SURVIVORS FOUND IN PAKISTANI PLANE

Most Victims in Saudi Air Disaster Were Returning from Mecca

RIYADH, Saudi Arabia, Nov. 26 (Reuters) — All 156 people aboard a Pakistan International Airlines jetliner

146 Britons Believed Dead in Crash Of Chartered Jet in Canary Islands

By The Associated Press

SANTA CRUZ DE TENERIFE, Canary Islands, April 25 — A chartered British jetliner with 138 British vacat and 8 crew mem aboard cr

Wreckage of the plane was sighted just before nightfall about 12 miles from the os Rodeos Airport outside Santa Cruz, contact was to land,

© 1979 and 1980 by The New York Times Company. Reprinted by permission.

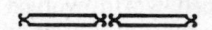

Théophraste Renaudot, publisher of the first newspaper in 17th-century France, one cannot do business with a city that has been destroyed.

When, in the 19th century, the invention of the steam-driven press and the further spread of literacy made it possible to publish newspapers in huge editions, publishers looked for mass audiences.

7

James Gordon Bennett, Jr. (1841–1918), called a "maharajah of journalistic sensation," took over the New York *Herald* from his father. Among his celebrated coups was sending Henry M. Stanley to Africa to find the lost missionary, David Livingstone (1871–72).

The Bettmann Archive, Inc.

They found they could attract readers by emphasizing dramatic events, human interest stories, and the foibles of well-known personalities, all presented in crisp, easy-to-understand language. In the case of foreign news, competing publishers vied in providing lurid accounts of battles and disasters, personalized stories about political intrigues and scandals, and items about snake charmers and witch doctors. News that was of significance to politicians and merchants was still supplied, but it now had to compete for space with news that could titillate a mass public.

But the mainstay of this "penny press" was local news: stories about city hall, crime, society, church activities. It has been said that James Gordon Bennett's New York *Herald,* founded in 1835, was the first newspaper to "cover" a city. He sent his reporters into the streets and to the law courts and treated gossip about prominent citizens with the same reverence that his predecessors had accorded to gossip about royalty.

This emphasis on local events persists in most newspapers and local television news programs. An advertisement published some years ago for the magazine of the Philadelphia *Sunday Bulletin* shows an editor in front of a blackboard talking to members of his staff. On the blackboard is his editorial instruction: "If it ain't local, forget it." But the text of the advertisement includes a significant qualification: "The problems of Afghanistan or Zanzibar are not in the magazine unless Philadelphians are involved and what is happening affects their daily lives. ..."

National media, including network television and newsmagazines, cannot emphasize local events as can media addressing an audience in a single area; but they, too, often look for ways of tying foreign news to the American scene. Thus, an event that takes place abroad may be reported mainly in terms of what a senator thinks about it; accounts of a civil war in another country may be concerned largely with the resident Americans who are affected, or with its impact on the American economy. On occasion, it is difficult to decide whether a given news item should be considered international or national news.

Most newspapers and broadcast news programs in the United States have adopted this practice of popularizing international news and attaching it to domestic interests, but what might be called the older tradition continues also. Travelers and scholars, diplomats and businessmen still provide reports about various aspects of the international scene. These are usually published in magazines with relatively small circulations, but some are included in radio or television interviews and documentaries, and some in national magazines. They constitute an important part of the available international news.

Today, what we call international news thus represents a crazy-quilt pattern of information about what is happening abroad mixed with reports about domestic reactions. It includes information regarding major economic, diplomatic, military or cultural developments, combined with human interest stories and reports about sports and disasters. It is chosen to entertain as well as to inform. Those who try to follow what is happening in the world often have to sort out substance from froth, significant events from the merely unusual.

Alternative Conceptions of International News

The picture we have drawn applies specifically to the United States, but its principal features are shared by the industrialized democracies of Europe and the Far East. There are, however, some differences. The press in many democracies is somewhat more responsive to governmental pressures than in the United States, and may soft-pedal news that would cause severe political embarrassment to the regime. On balance, media in some democracies are more "serious" in their treatment of international news than are most of the American media—although, as William Powell, who was the chief United Nations press spokesman for many years, comments, "every democracy has its serious and its frivolous press." It should not be assumed that the definitions of international news in any two democracies, as shown in their news media, will be exactly the same, even though they will share many important characteristics.

The news media of the Soviet Union, China, and other Communist countries offer a sharp contrast. As Mark Hopkins, Soviet affairs specialist for *The Milwaukee Journal,* wrote ten years ago, the Soviet press functions somewhat like the house organ of a large corporation. Its purpose is to serve the interests of the management (that is, the Communist party), to communicate instructions, cultivate good morale, and provide information necessary for carrying out the organization's plans. It has no obligation to report developments that are irrelevant to official policy; and those relevant events that are not in accord with policy are interpreted so as to appear as harmless as possible or, if not already common knowledge, are ignored.

Thus, criticism in the UN of Soviet intervention in Afghanistan was interpreted in the Soviet press as part of a conspiracy by American imperialists and Chinese hegemonists. Economic failures in the Soviet bloc are usually not mentioned unless the leadership wishes to launch a new policy or correct some widespread abuse. Weaknesses in the economies of the Western democracies, on the other hand, are regularly emphasized. The Soviet news agency TASS celebrated Thanksgiving Day, 1979, by citing statistics on poverty in the United States and commented that poor people, beaten down further by inflation, "have nothing to thank fate or Washington for on the official day of Thanksgiving."

Mao Zedong, the first leader of Communist China, neatly summarized the function of the press in a Communist state when he spoke to the editorial staff of a Chinese daily back in 1948: "The role and power of the newspapers consist of their ability to bring the party program, the party line, the party's general and specific policies, its tasks and methods of work, before the masses in the quickest and most extensive way." This philosophy, applied to both domestic and foreign news, leads to a definition of news as that information which the government wishes to have disseminated.

News treatment does differ among Communist states, however, just as it does among industrialized democracies. Some apply the criterion of what is useful to the government or party more loosely than others. The Chinese press has reported the world scene from a more varied perspective since the death of Mao. Rumanian, Hungarian and Polish newspapers frequently present information about international developments that is not available in the Soviet press, and the press in Yugoslavia is less rigidly controlled than in other Communist countries. Nevertheless, these are differences of degree rather than kind. The definition of news in all Communist states is rooted in Lenin's characterization of the press as a "collective propagandist, agitator, and organizer."

The "third-world" countries are an even more diverse group than either the Communist states or the Western democracies. Most of them, however, share a dissatisfaction with the way international news is defined in Western democracies, and they are now calling for a "New World Information Order." Their complaints have been heard with increasing frequency in the UN and other international forums.

Objections of third-world countries to the existing international information order are twofold: that much more news flows *from* the industrialized countries *to* the developing ones than in the other direction, and that what little news about developing countries reaches the world as a whole tends to be superficial, negative and distorted. Many spokesmen from the developing countries condemn the one-way flow as an intolerable form of "cultural domination" or "media imperialism." Those few reports about third-world nations that are circulated, they claim, tend to concern floods, famines, exotic customs or military coups; there is little news about progress in education, health or economic development.

Wide World Photos

Conflict is a main element in what U.S. media consider news. Example: Central America gets little U.S. news play except when there is trouble—as in the 1979 Sandinista revolt in Nicaragua.

If one can generalize about the wishes of this diverse group of countries, their main concern is that communication should play a positive role in helping them to develop their human and natural resources. The chief duty of the media, in this view, is not to inform but to assist. In 1979 a commission on international communication problems, sponsored by the UN Educational, Scientific and Cultural Organization and chaired by the Irish attorney, Sean MacBride, issued a report which stated this point of view as follows: "What communication can do is to focus attention, point out opportunities, attack indifference and obstruction, and influence the climate of opinion. Communication thus plays a supporting and participatory role in development, but its contribution can be significant. This applies both to the mobilization of public opinion in developing countries, and to the spread of greater understanding in the developed."

Developing countries place much of the blame for what they regard as the one-way, unbalanced flow of news on the four major Western news agencies—the Associated Press (AP), United Press International (UPI), Reuters and Agence France Presse. Not only are these the main channels for news about the developing nations in the media of the industrialized countries; they are also the main agencies on which citizens of developing countries have to rely for news about their neighbors and even about themselves.

Developing-country governments have already taken some steps to challenge the domination of these wire services by setting up a network of national news agencies and regional agencies. In 1973, the idea of a "third-world news agency pool" was presented at a conference of third-world countries in Algiers. Yugoslavia responded by offering the facilities of its national news agency, Tanjug, as a central point for the information pool, in which about 50 countries now participate. Other agencies with a third-world orientation include the Middle East News Agency (MENA), the Central American News Agency (ACAN) and the Caribbean News Agency (CANA).

The views of the developing countries about the proper conception of international news have not gone unchallenged. Western journalists who have examined the output of the third-world news agency pool have characterized it as heavily loaded with government press releases that show the world as officials of the developing countries wish it were, rather than the way it is. A leading authority on international communication, Wilbur Schramm, who compared the output of the Western international wire services with news published in the Asian press, concluded that the wire services were doing a fairly good job of reporting third-world news. The problem, he felt, was much more that the mass media in developing countries were not making proper use of the information that was available to them: "Reading the wires and the [Asian] papers, day after day, we felt that the picture of the third world on the wires was more full and more balanced than the picture we found in the newspapers."

Nevertheless, numerous Western journalists have expressed a degree of sympathy for the third-world view. *The Washington Post,* for example, editorialized in 1977: "One does not have to accept the third-world charges that Western news agencies are cultural and political predators in order to understand a country's reluctance to have its picture of the world, and the world's picture of it, drawn entirely by foreigners who are sometimes knowledgeable and sympathetic, sometimes not, but who nevertheless are foreigners."

The Difficulty of Seeing the Whole Picture

Our purpose in describing these complaints about Western news services and opposing conceptions as to the proper role of the press is neither to support nor to discredit them, but simply to emphasize that the ideas prevailing in other countries on this subject are quite different from our own. For the most part it is the Western ideas that determine the selection of news from these countries in our own media. Americans may be comfortable with the kinds of news thus selected for them; but we should realize that certain kinds of views and facts that do not fall within these Western conceptions tend to be screened out. Thus a person may be well informed by American standards about, for example, current events in Thailand or Nigeria, and still be quite ignorant according to the standards of those countries.

This is unfortunate, for to comprehend an international dispute it is necessary to look at the facts and issues as both sides see them. And what people on each side see is at least partly determined by the information that is available to them in their news media. It follows that one's understanding of international affairs can be greatly helped by gaining some knowledge of what the world looks like when seen through the eyes of other peoples and the news media of other countries.

It is difficult to gain such a picture, but an approximation is often possible. One can read background articles in addition to the "hard" news items. One can read the full texts of statements made by foreign governments (regularly distributed by their embassies in

Washington and at the UN)—not only stories *about* these statements. One can consult translations of materials from foreign publications, such as those presented in the monthly *World Press Review*. One can ask foreign visitors to describe the situation as they see it, and can keep one's eyes and ears open when traveling abroad. All this will help.

The definition of news commonly used in the United States may be the best one for us; we may even feel that it is the best for all nations; but nevertheless these other conceptions exist and can be a potent factor in the conduct of nations. Their existence—and the kind of information to which they give preference—is seldom clearly reflected in the news from abroad that is available to Americans. It is by no means easy to determine what facts about life in a foreign land are *not* reported in our media, what views are not presented; but, armed with a general awareness of these different conceptions, we can still sometimes imagine what these facts and views might be.

3
How Foreign News Is Covered

On the evening of February 20, 1980, the day the deadline ran out for Soviet troop withdrawal from Afghanistan if the United States were to participate in the Moscow Summer Olympics, viewers of the ABC-TV "World News Tonight" program watched an immediate reaction report from Moscow. Charles Bierbauer, ABC's Moscow correspondent, told what he expected the consequences of the American boycott to be and narrated scenes of Moscow taxi drivers in a classroom learning English for the expected crush of foreign tourists. The message was clear: the Russians were insisting that Olympic business would go on as usual.

To provide that kind of news coverage from the Soviet capital—even a short television item lasting only a few dozen seconds—is not as easy as viewers might suppose. Aside from the mechanics of deploying a camera crew, a problem peculiar to television, Bierbauer faced other problems common to correspondents for both broadcast and print media. First on the list is an uncooperative officialdom. The Soviet government does not regularly respond to correspondents' queries with newsworthy comments. News is a supplier's market in the U.S.S.R. If TASS, the Soviet news agency, or *Pravda*, the Communist party daily newspaper, wishes to make a statement, it does so, but at its own convenience, not that of the foreign press. Even in Moscow it is possible to get around this inflexible system through the use of confidential sources, as will be discussed later, but these sources cannot be produced on short notice.

Bierbauer has considerable qualifications for solving such problems. With long service as a correspondent in Germany, Yugoslavia and Austria as well as the Soviet Union, he knows how to plan ahead and how to deal with both officials and ordinary citizens. He is fluent in Russian and is a perceptive student of Soviet affairs. All these assets were important in producing his Olympics reaction story.

Especially for an electronic or wire service journalist, one of the most important working rules is constant contact with the home office or local or regional headquarters. Radio and television correspondents are on call for breaking news, or the reaction to breaking news, to meet a relentless series of deadlines day and night. Newspaper correspondents have to be concerned with making the

Wide World Photos

The Associated Press control desk in London, which disseminates world news to Europe and, via New York, to the entire Western Hemisphere

edition deadlines of their distant papers, and when major news is breaking the activity comes to an end only when the final edition has gone to press. It is a two-way flow of information: dispatches from correspondent to headquarters; ideas, suggestions, and other dispatches (for reaction) from headquarters to correspondent. And, as will be seen in chapter 4, the character of a correspondent's reporting is strongly influenced by what headquarters wants.

Events, Reactions and the Scene

In the foreign correspondent's pragmatic view, news can be roughly subdivided into three kinds of material. First, and of primary importance, are *events:* actions, happenings, statements, announcements or revelations, which occur within the reporter's assigned beat and are deemed worth writing about. Second, a considerable part of the news centers on *reactions*—statements, defensive steps, etc.—occasioned by events that have occurred in some other part of the world. Finally, there is *the scene:* a kaleidoscope of human interest and of the lives and opinions of ordinary folk in all walks of life, on which reporters draw to put flesh on the bare bones of political and governmental news. Some comment is in order on each of these kinds of material.

Events. Any event, if it is big enough, is likely to be international news no matter where it happens: a flood, a war, a world conference of heads of government, or a notable policy statement by a world leader. These are the hard news stories, the meat and potatoes of journalism. In its emphasis on them, foreign news differs in no degree from domestic news except that the event, being more distant, has to be bigger to be noticed.

Since journalists respond to events, public figures often go to some lengths to manage events—even to create "media events"—in ways that will put them and their policies in the best light. A leader of world rank, simply because of the power he wields, can hold a news conference in the certain knowledge that reporters will be on hand and that his words will be quoted and commented on (although not always in the way he desires) by the world media.

Sometimes a managed event turns out to be another news story entirely than that intended. A famous example is the coverage of the late Soviet Premier Nikita S. Khrushchev's visit in 1958 to an exhibition of American consumer products in Moscow with then

Vice President Richard M. Nixon. In the unscheduled "kitchen debate" that ensued, Nixon forcefully contested Khrushchev's views, advancing his political fortunes at home. Had not Robert Korengold of UPI, Osgood Carruthers of the AP, and other journalists been present for that debate, only the far less interesting official event would have been reported.

Similarly, but with far weightier results, the skepticism with which reporters like Malcolm Browne of the AP, Neil Sheehan of UPI, and David Halberstam of *The New York Times* greeted official U.S. attempts to "manage" news of the Vietnam war caused them to start reporting another kind of event—battlefield stories that ran counter to official claims of constant victories. And the history of diplomatic reporting is filled with instances of journalists ignoring the public sessions of international conferences and getting behind the scenes for revelations from participants that throw far more light on what is going on than the programmed announcements.

But many other "official" events are worthy of being reported as they occur; the drama on the center stage, even though predictable, is still overpowering because of what it represents. The signing of the Helsinki Final Act in 1975, Egyptian President Anwar el-Sadat's appearance before the Israeli Knesset in 1977, or the arrival in 1979 of Vice Premier Deng Xiaoping, the first Chinese Communist leader to visit the United States—these events, though carefully staged, were genuine news stories every bit as much as the Soviet invasion of Afghanistan or the starvation in Cambodia.

Reactions. Every day, reaction stories like Bierbauer's report from Moscow, described above, are filed by correspondents all over the world. Sometimes the news organization's headquarters, or its bureau in another country, suggests the reaction piece. Often the correspondent, keeping abreast of the news outside his or her bailiwick, does not need prompting. When President Lyndon B. Johnson announced his decision not to run for another term in the spring of 1968, Bernard Redmont, then a broadcast correspondent for Westinghouse, heard the news early in the morning on his shortwave radio in a Prague hotel room. Shortly after breakfast, he was sipping tea with diplomats at the North Vietnamese embassy in Prague. Redmont had close contacts with the Vietnamese in Paris and knew that the Prague embassy was an important link in the chain of Vietnamese missions in Eastern Europe. He also knew that no Western correspondents would be able to contact Hanoi directly. His authoritative quotes were the first reaction from a North Vietnamese source to be broadcast in the United States.

In situations of chronic conflict, such as the Arab-Israeli struggle, reaction stories are almost automatic—and new communications technology is making them more so. In March 1980, when President Carter disavowed the U.S. vote in the UN Security Council on Jewish settlements in the occupied territories, a many-sided pattern of reverberations could be discerned. With correspondents able in many cases to read each other's dispatches on video screens in their offices, and to call up previous accounts from computers, the reaction pattern moved from the UN to the State Department to the White House to Israel to Egypt, and then, with other voices from Europe, Capitol Hill, the American Jewish community and other countries of the Arab world joining in, went into still further rounds. Typically, a correspondent in the State Department pressroom would report a statement by the department's spokesman, and other correspondents along the line would take that statement to their own sources, official and unofficial, for comment. Soon a new comment would spawn further reactions—until a State Department spokesman would be constrained to make another statement, and the chain reaction would start over.

The Scene. This third type of material in foreign news serves an important need. It provides the descriptive color and human interest that can make a story on, say, irrigation or truck transport come to life and tempt readers into following and understanding a subject that otherwise would be dismissed as unimportant. Americans spend some $14 billion each year on travel to foreign countries, both to divert and to inform themselves; and yet some correspondents' reports leave out the very color and revealing details that attract travelers and, for the thoughtful reader, deepen understanding. Alastair Cooke, who has provided Britons with foreign correspondence from the United States for decades, considers color as important an element in his dispatches as any other, and uses quotations from the "man in the street" and descriptions of American life as context for the events he reports. When color predominates without relevance to the main theme, the travelogue effect sets in; hence it is important to keep a balance and a

One of the world's busiest centers of diplomatic news is the State Department briefing room in Washington. Hodding Carter III, the department's spokesman from 1977 to mid-1980, is shown talking to reporters during the U.S.-Iranian crisis, November 1979.

meaningful connection between substantive information and description. But, the more concretely the story is told the more likely it is to win attention—first from the editors who screen it and decide on its placement, and then from readers or viewers. Television reporters have the most effective means at their disposal: they need only the camera eye on their subject. Its impact can best be measured by the reporting of the Vietnam war—an important element in the national change of course.

Sources

Newsgathering in a foreign country is not a preprogrammed skill like flying an airplane; there are many different and equally acceptable ways of getting the news. Most correspondents make routine use of at least seven kinds of sources.

1. Officials. At noon of every working day, and at many other times of the day or night in times of crisis, a UN spokesman briefs correspondents at the UN headquarters in New York. The briefing can be routine and unproductive, or it can be laden with charges and countercharges that make news. Moreover, what seems routine is often recognized as important by the professional eye of a skilled reporter. Routine notice of an appointment with the UN secretary-general for the ambassador of a certain nation can speak volumes to a reporter who knows something about that nation's current involvement in a critical issue. And even if the briefing official is unwilling or unable to supply details of the meeting that ensues, there are, as will be discussed later, other means of learning.

Briefings—on the record, and open to all accredited reporters—are the setting in which officials are most accessible. But some of the most skilled journalists save their best questions for private visits or telephone calls to the officials to follow up topics touched on or to raise entirely new matters. This role for officials verges on another category which might be called—

2. Unofficials. A seemingly offhand remark at a cocktail party, or a private confirmation of a report that could not be acknowledged in public—these are methods often used by the official who, for any of a variety of reasons, wants a sensitive fact published without its source being revealed, and so acts in an unofficial capacity.

The needs for this role in government and diplomacy are manifold. To take the best-known instance, the "senior official traveling with the Secretary of State"—a phrase that began turning up in news stories during the Kissinger years—was a phenomenon the average reader was simply unable to understand. If the Secretary of State, whether Henry Kissinger or Cyrus Vance, was clearly the source, why not come out and say it openly?

As Jim Anderson of UPI, a diplomatic correspondent with long experience on the Middle East shuttles of both Kissinger and Vance, explained it, the simplest answer is that there is often something which the Secretary of State wants made public without, in effect, signing his name to it. An example might be his opinion on the delaying tactics of one of his negotiating partners in the Middle East. If it were pinned publicly on the Secretary, the party criticized might react by breaking off the talks. If a vaguer source is used, the hint may be taken in the appropriate quarters. Moreover, Anderson notes, the "senior official" has sometimes been just that: one of the Secretary's top aides. The veiled attribution keeps the public, and the negotiating partners, a little less sure of just who is speaking—thereby presenting a less obvious target for an angry public retort.

3. Diplomats, of course, are officials, but of a special kind, and especially interesting to reporters. Serving their various governments in someone else's country—or at the UN or other multilateral organizations—they perform the traditional foreign service duties of representation, negotiation and reporting. In all three capacities, and particularly the last, there is interest for the foreign correspondent. With its political, cultural, economic, and sometimes military divisions, a major embassy is a news- and information-gathering organization with vastly greater resources than those of even a large news bureau. Much of the correspondent's work consists of harnessing these capabilities to his or her reporting needs.

Two problems come up to interfere with this attractive relationship, one for each side.

For the foreign correspondent, there is danger in depending too much—in some cases solely—on a single embassy, usually that of his own country, for an account of events in the country they both happen to be in. The dependence of some correspondents on the official line from the vast American Embassy bureaucracy in Saigon during the Vietnam war, and the resultant loss of perspective, has been well documented. (With this experience in mind, a fourth function, propaganda—the dissemination of one-sided or misleading information—should perhaps be added to the duties of embassies, although just as often the embassy man may simply be a prisoner of the official bias and have no intention to mislead.) To counter such dangers, professional journalists do their best to check facts with some other source, preferably an adversary of the originator.

For the embassies, exchanging information with the correspondents can also be a mixed blessing. They benefit from the exchange, it is true: correspondents sometimes have access to sources, and go to places, that are off limits to diplomats, and can thus relay information not otherwise available to an embassy. But there is always the danger that information provided to a correspondent in exchange will wind up in public, with a not very diplomatic quotation from the talkative diplomat attached to it.

In order to prevent such embarrassments, with diplomats just as with other officials, an elaborate system of sourcing and attribution has been established. The details vary, but usually the scale runs from fairly penetrable attribution, such as "a European embassy official" or "a senior American diplomat," to what is called deep background, which can mean that no hint at all of the source's identity may be published. In each case an unwritten code, long accepted by both reporters and officials, gives the source the right to specify what attribution may be used.

Two elements are important in sourcing. The first is the protection of the source. No report or scoop, no matter how sensational, is worth the exposure of its confidential source. In any society, disapproval from the source's superiors would be the mildest result. In many societies, dismissal, imprisonment, or worse could follow. The reporter too has a strong interest in protection, since a confidential source, once exposed, is virtually certain to dry up.

The other element, often in conflict with the first, is the journalist's need to convince editors and readers that the information is true. Since it cannot be supported by statements like "President X told me today," it ought to be supported by the next best thing, in a sliding scale chosen to permit maximum credibility short of giving trouble or danger to the provider of the information. In some situations, the journalist might choose to give the source some protection even though the latter has not asked for it. In the turbulence of postinvasion Czechoslovakia in 1968, for example, one of the authors (Shanor) was given a whole series of on-the-record denunciations of the Soviet occupation by Czech and Slovak officials so angry that they were not worried about repercussions. He decided on his own to withhold their names—reasoning that readers would be less interested in names than in circumstances and sentiments, whereas the officials might very well regret having been so rash when the inevitable occupation crackdowns came. It was a decision that hurt no one and might even have helped some Czechs and Slovaks stay out of prison or exile.

4. Local journalists. During the "Prague Spring" of 1968, Czechoslovak press and television reporters were key information sources for the foreign correspondents. They were in the vanguard of the Communist party's reform movement and were eager to bring their side of the story to world attention.

Such a situation is not unusual. Even in an authoritarian state with a controlled press, foreign correspondents usually find local journalists far more approachable than, for example, academicians or novelists. There is a common language, even between those who work for the state press and those who represent an uncontrolled media system. There is also a good excuse for meeting: a new foreign correspondent in town can justify a courtesy call on the leading daily newspaper or official news agency, even under the tightest restrictions from the regime. Western journalists are taught in school, or at least learn in practice, that getting their news from other journalists isn't the most professional of working arrangements. It is far better to go to the primary source, consulting the local journalist only for a background briefing on the political situation and the best officials to try to reach.

That is a useful working rule for open societies. In closed societies, the rule may be justifiably suspended, since the primary sources are generally out of reach for the foreign correspondent. In Moscow, Beijing (Peking) or Tripoli, he is unlikely to be allowed—as reporters are in Washington, Bonn or London—to sit in on legislative hearings, go to court, attend news conferences in which officials may be pinned down with questions, receive background briefings and have access to data on the national budget, gross national product, and the like. But *local* journalists in closed societies do have at least some of these privileges, and thus become essential providers of missing ingredients in the information picture.

Such an arrangement calls for considerable mutual trust and discretion on both sides. If, as has sometimes happened, the helpful local journalist turns out to be a conduit for mere propaganda planted by the regime, the correspondent who trusted him will soon be in trouble and will thereafter shun this particular source. If the correspondent, on the other hand, is careless in his use of sensitive information, or fails to shield the identity of his source, the source will thereafter shun the correspondent—in time, it is to be hoped, to save his professional position and possibly his liberty.

With all these risks, why do the local journalists in authoritarian countries deal with the foreign correspondent at all?

An Egyptian journalist once explained to the author of this chapter his own attitudes about such contacts. He was, he said, as competent a reporter as any of the Westerners he dealt with. He was also better connected in his capital than they in theirs; for in Nasser's Egypt, as in many developing societies, the journalists were seen as one of the weapons in the arsenal of national development, and were part of the regime's team—not, as in Washington, skeptical observers and critics of the Administration. This meant that they were far more thoroughly briefed, even at the

25

highest level, than their Washington counterparts, and became privy to much fascinating information about cabinet sessions, international negotiations, possible coups and leadership changes—none of which had any chance of being published in the nation's controlled media.

Such a journalist, by imparting bits of his inside information to a foreign correspondent, can serve various purposes. He can get information published abroad in the hope that it will seep back into his own country. He can promote his own side in a factional power struggle. Or he can simply satisfy a frustrated human need to communicate what he knows. Whatever the motive, the foreign correspondent, if sufficiently discreet, benefits as a result.

5. The Opposition. One charge often leveled against the American media after an upheaval in a foreign country is that correspondents did not pay as much attention to the outs as to the ins, and as a result did not prepare their readers or viewers for what happened. If the charge implies a lack of diligence or enterprise, it is valid in some cases but not at all in others. The late Joe Alex Morris, Jr., correspondent in the Middle East for the *Los Angeles Times* until his death in the Iranian turmoil, was as familiar with the camps and side street offices of the opposition as he was with the chancelleries and palaces of governments in his area. Doug Tunnell, Arabic-speaking CBS correspondent in the Middle East, is similarly well connected. The list of others in this category is long.

How free a correspondent is to report to the outside world on such groups, however, is another matter. Very often the kind of repressive government that makes clandestine opposition necessary also restricts the opportunities of the foreign correspondent to deal with such groups. And if the correspondent does manage to elude the barriers to contact, there is always censorship or expulsion to keep the opposition message from getting out.

Even when the opportunity does arise to do a story on such a group, the facts can prove elusive. It is often hard to distinguish genuine dissident or liberation groups from café debating circles. Most seem to favor labels such as "national," "front," "liberation," and "army," whether they have a well-stocked armory and a large following or no more than a few adherents with pistols. Some groups make their presence felt by acts of terror, but these are no sure guide to their strength or standing. At this writing it is still difficult to gauge the true strength of the Iranian militants who seized the U.S. Embassy in Teheran, although they have received more attention from foreign correspondents than any other group since the Vietcong. To have pinpointed such a group and its potential before it struck would have been still more of a feat.

In sum, reporting on opposition movements in a dictatorship or a one-party state is an important but ticklish and often dangerous part of a correspondent's job. It would take a bold critic to second-guess an able correspondent on whether the journalistic benefits of tapping such sources outweigh the risks in a particular case.

6. The Man and Woman in the Street. Talking to ordinary people adds another dimension to foreign reporting, and the taxi driver in a foreign capital has become as hallowed a fixture as the maid dusting the furniture in the first act of a play. Taxi drivers often unknowingly convey important information about a society, as when they ask to be paid in dollars rather than in the local currency, or offer to change money at an astronomical rate. Moreover, drivers, porters, chambermaids and others who regularly serve foreign visitors are convenient sources—close at hand and, more often than not, able to speak the correspondent's language.

But as sources of information such people have their drawbacks. Often the views they express and the "facts" they report are colored by their experience of the benefits of telling the foreigner what he or she seems to want to hear. Besides, their fund of knowledge is limited. A taxi driver may be an excellent source on the price of gasoline or the movement of some official from hotel to ministry, but not on impending government shuffles or changes in foreign policy. Careful correspondents, knowing this, broaden their reporting on the average citizen to include people outside the tourist-hotel-airport run.

7. Nongovernmental and International. A final category of sources from which much information can be obtained consists of highly trained individuals in a miscellany of institutions present in nearly every country. These include university professors, UN advisers, businessmen, and members of scientific, research or cultural institutions. Such people are relatively easily accessible to correspondents. The information they supply is often missing from the official version of events—and not always because it is negative.

Sometimes the specialists can point to positive news that government officials may know little about. These may include, for example, development projects, usually located far from the capital city, under UN or other international sponsorship.

The business community provides not only news of its commercial transactions, but insights into the government and society that often are based on long experience and understanding. The same can be said of the personnel of scientific and social institutes and universities, even those of closed societies such as the Soviet Union. Studies and analyses done in these places are frequently not mentioned in the controlled press, but through cultivation and protection of sources, foreign journalists may have access to them.

Censorship

We have mentioned censorship as one of the impediments to foreign news coverage in many countries. The subject deserves further comment. The best foreign news story in the world has no meaning if no one is permitted to cover it, or if government censors can delete any mention of it. Such was the case, to cite one recent example, during much of the fighting in Afghanistan in the months following the Soviet invasion of December 1979. American correspondents were expelled, and the dispatches of those foreign journalists permitted to remain were subjected to heavy censorship.

A good idea of the two main forms censorship can take may be gleaned from an article by a *New York Times* Moscow correspondent, Anthony Austin. He had been a UPI correspondent in the Soviet capital in the 1950s, an era of strict official censorship, and returned at the end of the 70s to work under the new system.

"On the surface, things are freer," Austin wrote in 1980. No longer, he noted, is there direct censorship of outgoing news stories. Not for decades have correspondents' dispatches had to run the gauntlet of the Central Telegraph Agency on Gorky Street, where—with the reporter not even present to put up an argument—anything the censor found to be inconsistent with the official line would be struck out. That practice was abandoned during Khrushchev's destalinization period, and dispatches nowadays are transmitted out of Moscow uncensored.

"Yet to say that the regime permits free reporting from Moscow, as Soviet propagandists blandly insist, is to play with words," Austin comments. "To start with, a foreign correspondent is overwhelmed by the daily mass of disingenuous comment and pseudo-information which, being the voice of the Soviet Union, must be transmitted to his home office. He does his best to winnow the genuine from the mendacious and put it into proper context. Still, to a large extent, he ends up being used as a channel for the Kremlin's version of 'Soviet reality,' just as he was, and to an even greater degree, when censorship was in force."

Much the same story could be told of governmental censorship, direct or indirect, in many authoritarian countries where the regime habitually makes life difficult for a correspondent with a mind of his own. Even where foreign correspondents are free to send dispatches that could never be printed in the controlled press of the host country, a form of postcensorship may be practiced—often by expelling a correspondent, or even shutting down his bureau, if the regime takes offense at something his American employers have published.

Fireman Journalism: Good or Bad?

A different set of problems for foreign news coverage has been created by the news industry itself. It results from a recent tendency to cut down on the number of correspondents based in permanent news bureaus abroad, and to rely increasingly on less expensive—and less intensive—forms of coverage. Often, though not always, the result is superficiality.

The pressure in this direction is largely financial: the high and constantly rising cost of maintaining news bureaus in foreign countries. In a world of 4.3 billion people, for a U.S. news organization to maintain even one full-time correspondent abroad per 100 million people, for example, would require a permanent corps of over 40 correspondents. Of U.S. news organizations, only two substantially exceed this number. These are the two wire services on which most U.S. newspapers primarily depend for world news: the Associated Press and United Press International. Of the daily newspapers, *The New York Times* holds the lead with 30 or more full-time correspondents; next come the *Los Angeles Times* with 19, *The Christian Science Monitor* with 18, *The Washington Post* with 15 and *The Baltimore Sun* with 9. Of the commercial broadcasting networks, CBS has 14 full-time correspondents, NBC 15 and ABC 15. All, however, also employ some journalists on a part-time or free-lance basis.

Even in the largest news organizations, some bureaus have a regional rather than a one-country beat, with one or more correspondents based in a key capital covering events in a number of surrounding countries. This is especially true in the third world where, barring a crisis, most individual countries are not major day-to-day sources of news for the American media. A regional bureau's full-time staff may be supplemented in each country by the work of a local "stringer"—a free-lance journalist, often a national of the country in which he operates, who provides news coverage on request (frequently for more than one client) and is usually paid on a per-word or per-story basis. Stringers vary widely in the quality of their reporting. A few news organizations have long operated primarily through regional bureaus; others, like the Knight-Ridder newspaper chain, which had previously had no foreign bureaus at all, have recently adopted this system in a happy exception to the general downward trend.

Even the regional bureau system, however, is used by only a handful of the larger organizations. For others who want a less expensive means of firsthand coverage, the solution is to have one or two correspondents (as many as four in the case of the *Chicago Tribune*) with their bags more or less permanently packed, who act as "firemen"—flying to the hot spot of the day wherever it may be and staying for perhaps two days or a week while the crisis is at its height. The vast majority of U.S. newspapers and TV stations have no exclusive foreign coverage at all, and obtain what world news they see fit to publish from the major wire services and syndicates.

The trend toward fireman journalism has both advocates and critics. Satellite communications and the jet plane, editors argue, have made it far easier for the fire crew to go in from home base. And it is cheaper as well, considering the cost of living in most places that provide the bulk of the world's news. Critics, on the other hand, see a depressing pattern: a crisis in a distant nation, followed by the arrival of the press corps (often journalists who are unfamiliar with the country, the language and the issues), followed by saturation coverage until the crisis is over, followed by the departure of the press corps. It is a pattern that is repeated again and again in this era of civil wars and palace coups.

It would be simplistic to dismiss fireman journalism as the work of police beat or city hall reporters suddenly rushed to the airport and sent to a strange part of the world. Some have been of that caliber, but most have at least the experience of other crises behind them, and some, a good knowledge of the language and history of the areas they cover. Many defend the system as superior to sitting in a distant bureau for years waiting for something to happen. Moreover, a low budget need not always mean low quality: for example, the underfinanced Public Broadcasting System, using British and Canadian broadcast material and the American wire services as well as its own occasional correspondents, manages to get quality TV commentary on foreign news developments.

One current member of a fire brigade has had recent experience as a foreign-based correspondent as well. She is Shirley Christian, former AP bureau chief in Santiago, Chile, and now one of the three Latin American correspondents traveling out of Miami for *The Miami Herald*. The three divide their time between editing the daily Latin American and Caribbean page of the *Herald* and shuttling to crisis capitals like San Salvador and Managua.

"Quite frankly, I feel more comfortable writing about a country in which I am living or in which I have spent a great deal of time," Ms. Christian says. "Needless to say, I felt comfortable writing about Chile because I spent most of my time observing and thinking about what was going on there. I was also fond—in those days—of pointing out factual errors, or what I considered errors in judgment, in stories written by people who made short visits to Chile for the big U.S. newspapers and newsmagazines."

Ironically, in her new position she might seem to be doing the same kind of hit-or-miss roving correspondent job she used to scorn. But, she insists, she and her two colleagues are not just "chasing coups and earthquakes." Concentrating as they do on a single region, they have been able to acquire substantial knowledge about, and contacts in, the countries they cover. They write overall situation pieces that analyze basic trends, as well as exclusive hard news stories which sometimes take several days to put together. Their in-depth approach seems to show that a system of home-based foreign correspondents can be an adequate, if less than ideal, way of covering a complex and crisis-torn region. Still, even at its best, this system of in-and-out journalism has its limits. "If I could design an ideal foreign correspondent's job," Ms. Christian concludes, "I think it would be based in one large country and then devote about a third of the time traveling to, say, four or five smaller nearby countries. Traveling, as we do, to all of Latin America and the Caribbean is much more difficult to handle. I know this view goes against the current trend of SWAT journalism—fewer people but moving them about more because of technological improvements. Such people cannot help but know less about what they are covering."

John Chancellor of NBC agrees. In the Spring 1980 issue of *Foreign Policy*, in an article by Michael Mossetig and Henry Griggs, Jr., he is quoted as having said that the satellite technology now available to foreign broadcast correspondents helps them cover more news but hurts them in terms of depth.

Chancellor and the article's authors also agree that the new technology creates a new problem—the use of instant U.S. television broadcasts as a diplomatic lever by groups such as the militants in Iran. "We are becoming more vulnerable as they are becoming more skilled," Chancellor says.

Thus still another item has been added to the long list of obstacles that impede the gathering of foreign news. Those whose profession it is to cope with these obstacles—the few dozen correspondents in distant nations, and the editors and managements that undertake the cost and trouble of keeping them there—are entitled to a major share of the credit for setting before the American people as rich and well-balanced a diet of information and insight on international affairs as is available to any people in the world. How much of that diet most Americans actually consume, and what nourishment they derive from it, is another question, dealt with in the next chapter.

4
Delivering the News

At about 4 o'clock every weekday afternoon, network television news offices in New York become beehives of activity. Writers are beating out final texts on their typewriters, executive producers (who, together with the anchormen, are responsible for the final content of the newscast) are screening tapes that have just arrived from overseas. An associate executive producer may be on the telephone to London, checking what time a satellite broadcast will be available; another may be calling Washington to update a story from the White House. Aides are rushing in and out with copy from the wire service teleprinters. The question uppermost in everyone's mind, and especially in the mind of each executive producer, is: What stories should be included in the evening news program?

Earlier in the day, at a more leisurely pace, the news staff has made plans for the evening broadcast. Dispatches from the wire services have been reviewed, reporters have been given assignments, camera crews have been sent to cover expected newsworthy events, and the morning papers have been reviewed—especially *The New York Times* and *The Washington Post*. But the plans are continuously revised. Some stories work out; others don't. There is always so much more news than can be included that some tough last-minute decisions usually have to be made.

Somewhat the same scene can be observed at newspaper offices, but the news cycle is differently timed, depending on the hour at which the paper goes to press and the number of editions that are published. At many newspapers, the telegraph editor monitors the wire service ticker and decides what stories—both national and international—deserve space. On some major newspapers there is a foreign news desk which receives phoned-in or cabled stories from overseas correspondents, if the paper has any. These may be assigned to another journalist for rewriting; and they often are either cut or supplemented with other information.

At a predetermined hour—in the morning for afternoon papers; in the afternoon for morning papers—the heads of the various news desks meet. The foreign news desk may find it is up against stiff competition for front-page space, or even for space on the inside pages. National news may be more important that day, or the local news desk may have uncovered a lurid scandal in city hall. An executive editor or a managing editor makes the final decisions. The wastebaskets next to almost every editor's desk will be overflowing with stories that can't be used.

Of all those affected by this daily editorial conference, few are so vitally concerned as the foreign correspondent whose exertions were chronicled in the preceding chapter; for it is this group of editors who determine whether the story he has labored to produce will end up in the paper or in the wastebasket. "At bottom," comments Bernard D. Nossiter, a veteran *New York Times* reporter, "the correspondent writes not for history or the reader but a specific man, his editor. The correspondent will push his own perception just so far; if his stories are spiked [not used] or buried, he will respond to the unspoken pressure. He wants to be printed. So if the foreign editor is open, unbound by stereotype, genuinely eager for fresh ideas, the correspondent will reply in kind. If the foreign editor is a limited man or concerned with promoting front-page stories against rivals from other departments, the correspondent will be urged to harden and inflate his pieces, to seek sensation, to overplay conflict. A thoughtful editor gets a thoughtful report; a less scrupulous man does not."

The selection process for foreign news is simpler at smaller newspapers and at most radio stations. They usually subscribe to a service provided by AP or by UPI, which makes most decisions for them. The radio station may simply carry a news package prepared at a central point; and it is now possible for newspapers to have wire copy set in type electronically and printed without a local editor ever having touched it.

Selection by the Wire Services

A large proportion of the foreign news published in the American press is provided by the wire services, mainly AP and UPI. Some estimates range as high as 90 percent. But the news that actually is printed or broadcast is only a small part of what the wire services gather. The route from most overseas points to the teleprinters in the offices of subscribing newspapers and broadcasting stations is a long one, and more stories die than survive.

Let us take a hypothetical case. A wire service stringer in Bangkok learns that the Thai government is about to introduce a new family planning service. He cables his story to regional headquarters in Tokyo. The wire service editor there may decide that the story is of interest to subscribers in Asia, but not to those in North America. Or he may send it on to New York, but not until it is rewritten in briefer form.

In New York, another wire service editor looks at the story. He is not very impressed, but several other stories about family planning have accumulated from different points in Asia. So he assigns a writer to put them all together. The resulting story does not seem important enough to go to all subscribers in the United States, however, so it goes only to those news organizations that subscribe to the agency's feature service. Some editors decide to use it; others don't.

Although the two international wire services, AP and UPI, account for most of the foreign news that is published or broadcast in the United States, they are far from having a monopoly. Many news organizations subscribe also to the London-based Reuters agency; a few to the Paris-based Agence France Presse. In addition, there are half a dozen major news services offered by newspaper organizations: Los Angeles Times/Washington Post News Service and New York Times News Service are prominent examples. Through these services the work of outstanding foreign correspondents is made available to media that have no overseas correspondents of their own. They do not constitute a substitute for the comprehensive coverage of AP and UPI, but they can be a valuable supplement.

Additional international news reaches the media through specialized reporting agencies such as the Religious News Service. Syndicated columnists often have their own sources of foreign news. Guest columnists may include writers from abroad.

With these resources at his command, an energetic editor, even with a modest budget for foreign news, can still provide his audience with a diverse fare. Unfortunately, few do. Most allow their decisions to be made for them by the wire services, their major or sole suppliers of international news. They all pay close attention to the twice-daily news "budgets" of AP and UPI. These budgets, listing the topics and lengths of about a dozen top national and international stories, tell the editor what to expect. It is a rare editor who would completely ignore the budget and go on his or her own. So strong, in fact, is the mystique of the wire service budget that frequently a telegraph editor, seeing an item listed on it which strikes him as uninteresting, but not presuming to override the judgment of the AP or UPI, will run the gist of it as a two-inch item on page 1—thus giving it minimum space but high visibility.

How Much Is Printed or Broadcast?

The great majority of daily newspapers devote very little space to foreign news, even though enough foreign news to fill their news columns could easily be available to them. A typical paper will have one or at the most two stories dealing with international affairs on the front page. Inside pages may include as many as a dozen foreign news items, but some of these are likely to have little relevance to foreign policy: a train wreck in Africa, the birth of octuplets in South America, an earthquake in Asia. Syndicated columns may include more world news, but altogether there is not a great deal of significant information about what is going on in the world. Only the "big stories," as defined by the wire services, are carried prominently by most dailies.

A small number of newspapers, at the other extreme, provide voluminous coverage of foreign news. Most frequently mentioned as falling in this category are a handful of big-city dailies that maintain a substantial corps of full-time correspondents abroad: *The New York Times, The Washington Post, The Baltimore Sun,* the *Los Angeles Times* and the Boston-based *Christian Science Monitor.* These five also have full-time foreign news editors (or, at the *Monitor,* a managing editor with long experience as a foreign correspondent). There are a few other papers, published in both large and small cities, that provide much more foreign coverage than the average—often because of the interests of the editor or publisher rather than of the readership. And, as we saw in Chapter 3, *The Miami Herald* has developed a coverage of Caribbean and Latin American affairs that is unusual among newspapers in this country. *Newsweek, Time* and *U.S. News & World Report,* the three major newsmagazines, too, can be counted on for conscientious coverage of international news. They cannot match the level of detail in *The New York Times,* but provide far more information on what is going on abroad than the average daily.

Yet even the larger papers that emphasize international news tend to be highly selective, and conform to the common bias toward stories of conflict, and toward regions familiar to most readers, that we noted in Chapter 2. A recent study that sampled *The New York Times* during the period from 1960 through 1975 found that an average of 2.3 stories per day dealt with 18 countries in sub-Saharan Africa. The majority of these concerned the black-white conflicts in southern Africa, while most of the countries in this group were rarely mentioned. A study of Asian coverage in several major media during a randomly chosen week in 1977 disclosed a similar picture. Although the number of stories dealing with Asia was substantial—*The Washington Post,* for example, carried 47—nearly all had to do with crises or controversies in Japan, China, South Korea and Cambodia.

Historically, however, the long-term trend in newspaper coverage of world events may be upward. This, at least, is the implication of a 50-year study of foreign news trends in two Iowa dailies, *The Des Moines Register* and *The Cedar Rapids Gazette.* In 1914, *The Register* devoted 4.3 percent of its news space to foreign news; *The Gazette,* 3.8 percent. The proportion of space occupied by this

Anchorman Walter Cronkite, stopwatch in hand, puts finishing touches on copy for the daily half-hour CBS Evening News show.

CBS News Photo

category of information grew steadily in both papers, ballooning to over 30 percent during World War II. As of 1964, the figure for *The Register* was 10.4 percent, and 11.6 percent for *The Gazette*— much more than twice what it had been in 1914. This growth is all the more impressive, since the amount of space available for news of all kinds had nearly doubled during the 50-year period. It is probable that the space devoted to international news has remained constant or increased slightly since the study was completed in 1964.

In contrast to the daily newspaper, network television can cover a far smaller number of stories in each evening news broadcast (usually 15 to 20), and can devote fewer words to each. Nevertheless, a large proportion of the items presented on network news programs can be classified as international news. The number of such items naturally varies according to the state of international relations. During 1972, for example, when Vietnam was in the news, all three networks averaged about seven foreign news items per program. In the following two years, the average sank to between five and six. In 1975, a year of many crises, the average rose again to about seven.

With room for so few items on each evening news show, many important parts of the world have to be slighted. During a four-year period, 1972 to 1975, half of the countries of the world were not dealt with at all by network television news. On one network, the only African country receiving more than a dozen mentions was Egypt, with 41; the only Latin American country with an appreciable number of mentions was Cuba, with 13. The People's Republic of China received 39 and Japan 32. The most attention went to the Soviet Union, Vietnam, Israel, France and Britain, with a combined total of almost 700 mentions. The other networks showed a similar pattern.

Occasional documentaries, television "magazine" segments, locally prepared news programs, and interview programs provide additional international coverage. All in all, however, commercial television, whatever its advantage in pictorial vividness, cannot compete with a major newspaper in the extent or depth of its treatment of world news.

Newsmagazines, and those newspapers that stress foreign coverage, carry about ten times as much foreign affairs information as television, radio and locally oriented newspapers, but even they feel a need to be very selective. In general, editors who are responsible for the selection say they present as much international news to the public as the public will accept. Indeed, many editors are convinced that most of their foreign coverage is unheeded, except by a small minority. They include it out of a sense of professional responsibility but have little hope that it will find a wide audience.

Supplementary Sources

Those who want more information about international affairs than can be obtained from the major commercial mass media can turn to an enormous number of supplementary sources. Among the most important is public television, which now can be received in about 75 percent of all American homes. Its audience share is still very small in most areas. The MacNeil/Lehrer Report, which devotes half an hour each weekday evening to the analysis of a single topic, deals with some aspects of world affairs in more detail than any commercial television program except occasional documentaries. Public TV also presents commentaries by numerous academic specialists on various facets of foreign policy.

Similarly, National Public Radio, with participating stations in over 200 communities nationwide, presents substantially more international news and discussion programs than the commercial networks. Its daily hour-long program "All Things Considered" devotes an average of 15 minutes to news and commentary on international affairs.

Short-wave radio broadcasts from foreign countries are a source of information about international affairs that is relatively little used, although its audience in the United States is greater than one might think. Projections from sample surveys indicate that about 1 million people regularly tune in to one or more short-wave programs from abroad at least once a week. Recent improvements in short-wave receivers may lead to an increase in the size of this audience. Although listeners have to allow for the biases of different governments which do most of the broadcasting, much can be learned from this source about foreign points of view.

Brownie Harris, New York, and WNET/THIRTEEN

Public TV, with a smaller audience more attuned to foreign policy, can cover world affairs in more depth than the commercial networks. Here Robert MacNeil talks with Andrew Young, then the U.S. ambassador to the UN.

Conversations with foreign visitors in the United States and with Americans returned from overseas are another source that is available in almost every community. Although the listener must be able in each case to gauge how objective and observant the speaker is, such people can often supply points of view and background facts that are useful in interpreting what appears in the news media.

The richest store of supplementary information about international affairs is to be found in books and periodicals. While most serious books on history and contemporary life of other nations have a very limited readership, they are easily available in the larger public libraries. Among periodicals of value in this sense, some—such as the *Saturday Review, The Wilson Quarterly, The New Yorker, The New Leader* and *The Nation*—publish numerous articles and items on international subjects along with other matter. Their circulations range from a few tens of thousands up to over half a million. The more specialized journals devoted principally or wholly to world affairs have a smaller readership. The *Standard Periodical Directory* lists over 1,000 such periodicals published in the United States and Canada. Most of these deal with a limited segment—Japan, diplomatic history, arms control, the Middle East, etc.—and many are written in technical language. A number,

Reni Photos

NBC News anchorman John Chancellor interviewed Egyptian President Anwar el-Sadat for the *Today* show, April 1980—an example of network spot coverage of world affairs in addition to the evening news.

41

however, are more readable and cover the whole range of world affairs. *Foreign Affairs,* the quarterly published by the Council on Foreign Relations, is the giant of this latter category, with a circulation of 75,000 copies. Its rival, *Foreign Policy,* published by the Carnegie Endowment for International Peace, has a circulation of 20,000 copies. *The Inter Dependent,* a monthly published by the United Nations Association of the United States, reached some 30,000 subscribers before its publication was suspended in 1979. The monthly *Current History,* each issue of which deals with a single area, reaches 26,000. Issues of the HEADLINE Series, in which this essay appears, have an average lifetime paid distribution, by subscription and direct sale, of 12,000 or more. Most other periodicals in the field have smaller editions.

Among the more specialized publications dealing with foreign affairs, journals devoted to international trade occupy an important place. Some 400 of these are published in the United States and Canada. They include periodicals issued by foreign governments, such as *Italian Trade Topics,* which has a circulation of about 20,000, and *Japan Report,* with about 8,000. Others are published by private organizations concerned with international commerce or by commercial publishers. While focusing on economic matters, they include considerable information on political and cultural affairs as well.

Judicious use of supplementary sources, combined with attention to television, radio and newspaper reports, makes it possible for those who are interested to build up a more complete picture of world affairs than has ever been possible before.

This does not mean that the available information is of the highest quality. One can argue that news media do not cover all of the most significant developments, and that many supplementary sources are biased, or concerned with too narrow a range of information, or both. But the fact remains that, as a society, we have far more information about international affairs available to us than we know what to do with.

5
Audiences for International News

Information about world affairs is available to almost everyone through television, radio and the printed media. But some members of the public pay little attention to it. Others are interested in certain categories of the news: stories about dramatic events, reports about developments that may affect them personally or, perhaps, news about their country of origin. Still others are concerned with U.S. foreign policy in general and consume a wide range of international news. This group is often called the foreign policy attentive public. There are thus several audiences for international information; not just one.

All these audiences affect the world affairs content of the mass media. The inattentive exert a depressing influence, since editors are reluctant to devote scarce space or time to content that is likely to be ignored. Those with special interests encourage the media to cover some subjects or areas more intensively than others. Members of the foreign policy attentive public frequently complain that the mass media provide inadequate coverage of international news.

Lines dividing the various audiences are blurred. Individuals move from one group to another as their circumstances and interests change. During wartime and other times of international crisis nearly everyone may become concerned with some aspects of foreign affairs. The fact that the mass media are available to the total population means that, in theory at least, any person who wishes to learn about major foreign policy issues can become a member of the attentive public.

Attention to Major News Sources

According to a recent survey conducted by the Roper Organization for the Television Information Office, Americans 18 years and over typically spend three hours and eight minutes per day viewing television—up more than half an hour in the past 15 years. The corresponding figure for those with a college education is two hours and thirty-one minutes.

As television viewing has increased, so has the proportion of those who say that they get most of their news from television. Here are the survey results for 1968 and 1978 on "where you usually get most of your news about what's going on in the world today":

	1968 Percent	1978 Percent
Television	59	67
Newspapers	49	49
Radio	25	20
Magazines	7	5
Talking to people	5	5

Percentages add to more than 100 because some respondents named more than one source.

Newspaper publishers have not taken these findings lying down. They have responded with their own surveys, but have used different questions. In 1977 the Newspaper Advertising Bureau asked a national cross section of people aged 18 and older whether they had watched a television news program, heard a radio newscast, or read a newspaper "yesterday." The results showed newspapers slightly in the lead, but also showed—as do many other surveys—that most people rely on more than one of the media:

	Percent
Newspapers	69
Television news programs	62
Radio newscasts	49
All three sources	25
Only one source	28

Percentages add to more than 100 because some respondents named more than one source.

Three other research findings on Americans' use of the news media are worth noting. One is that about half the people who watch TV news do not watch a network news program, but a local one. International news, of course, is less plentiful on the local programs.

A second finding is that the more highly educated people are, the more likely they are to read a daily paper—but the differences, at least at the college graduate level, are not great. In a 1973 study sponsored by the American Newspaper Publishers Association, for example, 88 percent of college graduates were found to read one newspaper on an average weekday, while 77 percent of all adults did so.

Finally, it is interesting to note that, according to a 12-nation survey sponsored by a UN agency, urban and suburban Americans in the mid-1960s spent more time each day *both* in watching TV (92 minutes on the average) *and* in reading newspapers (24 minutes) than their counterparts in any other country studied. Following are average daily exposure times (in minutes) to several media in four leading countries:

	United States	West Germany	France	U.S.S.R.
Radio	4	7	5	10
Television	92	63	58	38
Newspapers	24	12	14	15
Magazines	6	12	4	5
Books	5	6	7	29
Movies	3	3	3	15

Source: Alexander Szalai, editor, *The Use of Time: Daily Activities of Urban and Suburban Populations in Twelve Countries*. The Hague and Paris, Mouton & Co., 1972.

Interest in International News

Americans, then, spend a good deal of time with the mass media, and there is evidence that much of this time is spent in watching, reading or listening to the news. But how much attention do they pay to *international* news? One clue to the answer is provided by a question that has been asked regularly by the Gallup Poll for more than 40 years: "What do you think is the most important problem facing this country today?" Over the years, some aspect of foreign affairs has been seen as most important more than half the time. At other times domestic issues—inflation and unemployment, labor unrest or race relations, at one point even the Watergate scandal—led the list. During World War II the main problem was "winning the war"; in 1951 and 1952, the Korean war; from 1953 to 1963, "keeping the peace"; from 1964 to 1972, the Vietnam war. In 1979, when American Embassy personnel were taken hostage in Iran, the world situation again became the primary concern.

More direct evidence of public interest in foreign news can be seen in the results of a survey sponsored by the Knight-Ridder Newspapers in the southeastern United States in 1975. In a rating of people's interest in 19 different categories of news, world events scored highest with 58 percent calling themselves "very interested"—outpacing national politics (55 percent), consumer information (54), local issues and politics (47), crime and big cities (47), food (42), college sports (37), rearing children (36), gardening (33), how to cope with modern life (29) and travel (24).

But it is one thing for people to *say* they are interested in news about international events; whether people actually pay attention to such news is something else again. Most journalists tend to be pessimists about public attention to foreign news. On the surface, there seems to be a direct conflict between journalists and the public on this point. In 1977, the Harris Poll raised the question not only with a national cross section of the public but also with 162 leading editors, news directors and reporters. Only 5 percent of the journalists thought the public was greatly interested in international news, while 41 percent of the general public said they were interested. In contrast, three-quarters of the journalists thought the public was very interested in sports news, but only 35 percent of the national cross section actually expressed such an interest.

Who is right? Probably both sides are, but they are thinking about different things. Uppermost in the editors' minds may be the large daily inflow of dispatches from all over the world which they receive from the wire services, most of which they do not print. Members of the public are likely to be thinking about the big stories having to do with war and peace, crises and revolutions.

Indeed, there is some evidence that the volume of foreign news that U.S. newspapers actually carry—at least on subjects where American lives are not at stake—may be somewhat more than the average reader's appetite would justify. Such, at least, is the implication of a 1973 study by the American Newspaper Publishers Association. It determined the relative *frequency* of international and diplomatic news items appearing in a selection of newspapers, and compared this with the relative *popularity* of this category of news, gauged by actual readership. The same was done for three other news categories. For each category, a score of 100 would have meant that the percentage of all readers who looked at items in that category was exactly proportionate to the relative frequency of such items in the paper. A score above 100 meant that readership exceeded this level; below 100, that it fell short. The four categories and their scores were: crime, 136; the Vietnam war and other wars then in progress, 113; U.S. government and domestic affairs, 112; international and diplomatic, 89—a poor fourth.

The Newspaper Advertising Bureau's 1977 study of how the public gets its news arrived at similar conclusions. It ranked readership of international news in second place, well behind local and national news, but ahead of cultural news and stories about business and finance.

Furthermore, when respondents in this survey were asked, "What was the biggest thing in the news yesterday or today?" only about one in twenty, or 5 percent, mentioned an international event. The interviewing was conducted during a week in March 1977, when Zaire was invaded by rebel forces, Indian Prime Minister Indira Gandhi faced defeat in an election, and President Carter gave a controversial speech about the Palestinians and also received Japanese Prime Minister Takeo Fukuda at the White House. In contrast, 22 percent remembered a story dealing with crime, and 18 percent referred to items dealing with national affairs.

It would thus appear that, for most consumers of news, international news is recognized as important—in principle; but unless it is truly earthshaking it takes a back seat to several other news categories.

Knowledge About Foreign Affairs

Whether or not people pay attention to stories about international events, the bottom line is how much they learn. Here, again, the evidence is somewhat conflicting. On the one hand, opinion researchers continue to unearth shocking cases of public ignorance; on the other, most people are aware of major international problems affecting the United States and have opinions about them.

Examples of ignorance have been plentiful ever since regular public opinion polls began to be conducted. Shortly after Dag Hammarskjold was appointed as the new secretary-general of the UN in 1953, only 10 percent of the respondents in a national poll could recall his name. Yet it had been prominent in the news media for some time. In December 1961 only 13 percent were able to say what the European Common Market was. And so on.

Yet, over time, people do learn. In 1975, when the Opinion Research Corporation asked a national cross section what country "owns the Panama Canal and the Canal Zone surrounding it," 35 percent could give the correct answer. Even more (44 percent) said they didn't know; 14 percent thought it was owned by Panama; some even thought it was owned by Arabs, Israel or Cuba. By January 1978, however, after the controversial treaties with Panama had been debated in the news media for several months, about three-quarters of the public was aware of the debate, and more than half could cite some of the provisions of the treaties.

Similarly, the popular level of information about Vietnam was very low in the early 1960s, prior to the large-scale involvement of American troops there. Public familiarity with the Vietnam situation steadily increased, and by the spring of 1967 more than two-thirds of a national cross section reported discussing the Vietnam situation with other people (almost as many volunteered that they thought it was the most important problem facing the country), and 13 percent said that they had tried to change someone else's opinion. About 2 percent had written to some official on the subject of Vietnam.

The picture of public information that these examples suggest is one in which most people remain fairly ignorant about international affairs until a crisis arises or a major decision has to be made. Then large numbers become informed of some details—enough, at least, to enable them to engage in discussions on the subject.

Lack of very much information does not always prevent people from having opinions, however. In opinion polls, the number who can be considered well informed is nearly always smaller than the number who are willing to come out on one or another side of an issue. This is partly because polltakers often briefly provide some essential facts about a question before asking for an opinion on it. For example, on two occasions during 1977, the Gallup Poll asked members of a national cross section if they had "heard or read about the situation in the Middle East." Those who said Yes—on one occasion 86 percent and on another 79 percent—were then given a one-sentence briefing: "As a result of the 1967 war, Israel now controls land that was formerly controlled by Arab nations," followed by this question: "What do you think Israel should do—give back part of this land, give back all of this land, or keep all of this land?" In spite of the complexity of the problem, three-quarters of those polled had an opinion about what should be done. (On both occasions, about 35 percent said "give back part," about 15 percent said "give it all back," and about 25 percent said "keep it all." The rest gave no opinion.)

Yet the willingness of so many people to take a stand on an issue is clearly not due entirely to the mechanics of polltaking. It seems to result in part from a feeling that one *should* have an opinion, and from the fact that relatively little information is needed if one is to form a preference. Opinions formed in this way are, however, likely to change as circumstances change or as more information is absorbed. During presidential primary campaigns, the popularity of relatively unknown candidates can fluctuate wildly, driving polltakers to despair.

'Know-Nothings' and 'Know-It-Alls'

In 1964, the Survey Research Center of the University of Michigan carried out a study of attitudes toward mainland China. At that time, the United States recognized the government on Taiwan as the only legitimate Chinese government, and kept the Communist regime on the mainland in diplomatic limbo, but many observers had long questioned the wisdom of this policy.

To ascertain the level of information of respondents, the researchers included four "knowledge" questions in the survey:

1. Do you happen to know what kind of government most of China has right now—whether it's democratic, Communist or what?
2. Have you happened to hear anything about another Chinese government besides the Communist one?
3. Do you happen to know whether the United States has been treating Russia and China the same up to now, or whether we've been treating them differently?
4. Have you happened to hear anything about the fighting in Vietnam?

The average number of "correct" responses varied widely according to the economic and social status of the respondents. The most disadvantaged category—nonwhites with less than a high school education and a family income of under $7,500 a year—averaged less than one correct answer out of a possible four. At the other extreme, college graduates in white collar occupations averaged 3.6 correct answers. (It is important to note, however, that some individuals with low incomes and little education did prove to be rather well informed.)

Other studies have shown substantially the same linkage between economic and social status and knowledge of international affairs. A Survey Research Center study in Detroit, also in 1964, asked 16 questions about characteristics of countries throughout the world. It found that the most disadvantaged group could answer only an average of three questions correctly, while the group at the other end of the scale averaged 12.

Do these different levels of knowledge have anything to do with differences in exposure to the news media? The answer appears to be Yes—but with respect to the print media only. As for broadcast news, the Detroit survey, and others as well, shows that the percentages of those who regularly watch TV news programs are equally high at all educational and economic levels, and the smaller percentages of radio news listeners also show little variation. On the other hand, the percentage of those who regularly read the news in daily papers rises substantially as economic and educational status rises, just as does knowledge about international affairs. The rise is still more striking for magazines:

Education and Sources of World News
(Detroit, 1964)

	Percentage who regularly obtained news from—			
	Magazines	Newspapers	Radio	TV
People with less than high-school diploma and low income	4	47	48	91
High-school graduates with incomes over $4,000	21	60	49	92
College graduates in white collar occupations	50	75	57	91

Percentages for each educational level add to more than 100 because most respondents had more than one source.

As these findings suggest, the popularity of television does not necessarily reduce newspaper readership. Indeed, other studies show that people who watch television news are likely to spend a little more time reading newspapers. And afternoon newspapers have made their best circulation gains since 1970 in markets where television newscast ratings are highest. Among those with more education, television seems to produce a demand for more information, to be found mainly in the print media.

A number of journalists working in television have suggested that this is an important function of television—to serve as a headline service that alerts the public to important developments. But having alerted, TV is much less able to satisfy the demand for more. Peter Sturtevant, national news editor of CBS-TV, was quoted in *TV Guide* as saying: "All we can do is whet people's appetite.... It's frightening to think that so many people rely on TV as their primary or sole source of news. If that's the case, they aren't very well informed."

The Active Foreign Policy Public

Those who, day in and day out, take an active interest in world affairs are too few to be captured reliably by public opinion polls.

By Auth for The Philadelphia Inquirer

'I HAVE A TICKET TO THE PRESIDENT'S TOWN MEETING, BUT I THINK I'LL STAY HOME AND MONITOR THE CRISIS IN IRAN.'

Members of the educated "attentive public" pay far more attention to foreign news than most people. Among the attentives, a still smaller number of activists require a copious diet of foreign news as background for their efforts to influence policy.

They are people who espouse foreign policy causes ranging from peace in the Middle East to saving the whales; who advocate their views by writing letters to the editor, communicating with officials in Washington, taking part in public hearings and conferences on foreign policy issues, and so on. Only a modest percentage even of the foreign policy attentive public belongs to this active group.

Members of the active foreign policy public not only consult more sources of information on international affairs than most people; they also use sources that are richer in information. In particular, a large proportion of them regularly read newspapers that give more information about world affairs than the average daily. For example, 67 percent of those who attended a national conference on foreign aid in 1958 were *New York Times* readers. A survey of business leaders made a few years earlier found that 30 percent of a national sample said that they regularly read *The Times*. And a 1974 study that sampled the top officials of political, economic and other major institutions in the United States found that *The New York Times, The Wall Street Journal* and *The Washington Post* were the preferred newspapers of this influential group, many of whose members take a keen interest in foreign policy.

Many members of the active foreign policy public also supplement their diet of news by reading specialized magazines, books and reports, and through personal communication with informed people. The few thousand scholars who specialize in international affairs may read a dozen or more journals devoted to particular parts of the world or to specialized aspects of foreign policy. Business people may rely more on government economic reports, newsletters, and memoranda prepared to meet their special needs. Those with more general interests may read such periodicals as *Foreign Affairs, Foreign Policy* and the London *Economist,* or the publications of the Foreign Policy Association. Those who feel a need to keep up with foreign points of view may read one or more of the best newspapers published abroad, or else sample foreign commentary in the American monthly *World Press Review.*

Opportunities to interact with others who are well acquainted with the international scene occur in the course of foreign travel, meetings with foreign visitors in the United States, attendance at lectures and participation in special programs, such as the Foreign Policy Association's Great Decisions program or university extension courses. In general, those who have one such source of information tend to have others as well. Thus, the opinion ballots returned by people who participated in Great Decisions discussion groups in 1978 showed that, during the preceding year, 25 percent had entertained foreign visitors in their homes; 29 percent had traveled abroad within the past 12 months; and two-thirds said they followed foreign news fairly regularly in the press. The incidence of reported conversations about international affairs also increases as one moves from the less-informed sectors of the population to the best-informed.

Just how large is the group of those who, year in and year out, take an active interest in foreign policy? Estimates range, depending partly on how the terms are defined, between 1 million and 2 million persons, or roughly 1 percent of the adult population. The number rises when the United States is involved in war or in a serious international crisis, and members of ethnic minorities may become active when the interests of countries with which they identify are at stake, but we are more concerned with those for whom foreign policy is a continuing preoccupation. These are the people who spend the most time following international affairs in the news media, and they learn the most in doing so, for they have acquired from many sources a richer background of knowledge and ideas than the average citizen and hence a greater ability to find significance in a given item of news. Moreover, in the network of communication on world affairs, many of these people are not only receivers; they are also sources. Their ranks include journalists, publishers, active and retired government officials and military officers, business and professional leaders, heads of organizations, educators—people who speak or write about foreign affairs, whose views are listened to, and who can often affect public attitudes and sometimes even policy decisions in Washington. Their influence in foreign affairs is far beyond their numbers.

Can the Active Foreign Policy Public Be Expanded?

A number of efforts have been made over the years to increase the size of the attentive foreign policy public, to encourage more members of this public to become active, to improve the quality of its attention, and to obtain more and better coverage of international affairs both in the news media and in public education. Since the public and the media influence each other in highly complex ways, it is no easy matter to decide at what point to attack the problem. Should we educate the public so as to improve the news media, or improve the media in order to educate the public? Both approaches have been tried. The basic reasoning in all cases, however, has been that more and better information and education would produce a public better informed on foreign policy issues, more attentive to world affairs, and less susceptible to narrow or demagogical appeals; and that from this improvement a more enlightened foreign policy would result.

One suggested approach is to increase and improve foreign affairs education in schools and colleges. Whether such efforts can significantly enlarge the active, well-informed foreign policy public is not definitely known. There has been a rapid increase during the past generation in the proportion of Americans who have attended college and thus, in most cases, have been exposed to at least some learning relevant to an understanding of world affairs. Perhaps it is too soon to trace concrete results in increased public sophistication about international issues. This road to an informed public is one that will, at best, take many years to travel.

A second type of approach calls for increasing the amount of information on world affairs in news media and the community at large. Numerous efforts have been carried out along this line, some of them consisting of experiments limited to one community and to a specific time frame.

One such experiment was conducted in Cincinnati, Ohio, in 1947-48 when the then American Association for the United Nations, together with its Cincinnati affiliate and the Stephen H. Wilder Foundation, embarked on a campaign to make people in the Greater Cincinnati area conscious of the UN. The broader aim was to demonstrate, as the sponsors put it, "how a community may become so intelligently informed on world affairs as to be a dynamic force in the creation of an ordered and eventually a peaceful world."

The campaign lasted six months, during which local citizens were deluged with information about the world organization. Mass media, advertisers, schools, religious groups and civic bodies cooperated in disseminating facts about the UN, including the slogan of the campaign: "Peace begins with the United Nations—the United Nations begins with you." Advertising posters displayed the message in buses; newspapers increased their coverage of the UN, thousands of matchbooks and blotters with the campaign slogan on them were distributed, and one radio station scheduled as many as 150 spot announcements about the UN each week.

This vigorous effort had a scarcely discernible impact. A survey by the National Opinion Research Center, prior to the campaign, found 30 percent of the population almost totally ignorant of the purposes of the UN. This percentage was essentially unchanged in a second survey conducted after the campaign was over. One respondent, questioned afterward about the campaign slogan, said: "Why, yes, I heard it over and over again. . . . But I never did find out what it means."

A rather similar experiment was conducted in Findlay, Ohio, in the early 1970s under the auspices of the Charles F. Kettering Foundation. There were good reasons to believe that the Findlay

Community Awareness Project, as it was officially known, would be more successful than the effort in Cincinnati had been. Findlay is a small city of 36,000, where most people both live and work in the community. The residents tend to be well educated and reasonably prosperous. Furthermore, the project concentrated on increasing person-to-person communication about international affairs, rather than relying mainly on the local mass media, since research during the 25 years since the Cincinnati effort had indicated that information people obtain from other people tends to have a greater impact than information from print and broadcast sources.

Fifteen individuals, chosen for their positions and leadership skills, were initially enlisted in the program. They included a newspaper editor, the general manager of a radio station, a vice-president of the local college, and several other educators, business people, government personnel, and civic leaders. This core group participated in intensive seminars on national development in Tanzania and Kenya and in other self-education activities. Then, in the summer of 1973, they journeyed to East Africa for a three-week visit. On their return, they planned and carried out more than 30 informational projects during an 18-month period. These included special radio and television programs, newspaper articles, over 100 speaking engagements, community seminars, and teacher inservice workshops. The radio station broadcast a series of 20 programs dealing with development issues in East Africa. The local newspaper sent a reporter to UN conferences on food and population in Rome and Bucharest and published the stories that he filed directly from Italy and Rumania.

To find out what all these efforts achieved, surveys were conducted among the people of Findlay before the information projects began and again after they ended. (To screen out any changes induced by extraneous factors, the same surveys were also conducted in a "control" city, Marion, Ohio, where no information campaign was carried out.) The surveys did indeed show that some changes had occurred in the target population. These included changes in patterns of newspaper readership, in perceptions of world interdependence, and in awareness of the plight of the poor in other countries. But the changes were rather small, and no significant changes at all appeared in many of the other characteristics that were tested. The sponsors concluded that the project had not lasted long enough and should have been backed up by a local organization that would keep interest alive. An undercurrent of disappointment can be detected in the final report.

Yet, in one respect, both the Cincinnati and the Findlay experiments could be considered quite successful. They both strengthened the active foreign policy publics in their respective locations. In Cincinnati there were numerous indications that those who were already interested in and informed about the UN became even more interested and better informed as a result of the campaign. In Findlay, there was a striking impact on the attitudes and level of information of the 15 members of the core group itself. They developed a greater sense of the interdependence of nations and felt more strongly that the United States should help other countries to grow and develop. A small number of other Findlay residents also showed significantly more involvement in world affairs.

It would thus appear that the *quality* of the active foreign policy public can be enhanced by increasing the amount of available information about international affairs, even if the *size* of the public may be only slightly affected. More and better information in the news media and in other sources enables those who are already interested and active to become better informed. They can make more sophisticated judgments and can participate more effectively in the foreign policy debate.

# 6

Conclusion: The Media and the 'Active' Public

Critics of the American media have often denounced them for emphasizing conflict, reporting trivialities, ignoring the underlying forces that shape events, and numerous other derelictions. In contrast, a group of prominent journalists and students of international communication, meeting in 1979 under Stanley Foundation auspices, concluded that "American media coverage of international news is among the best in the world and may be better today than it ever has been."

Whatever position one takes on this question, it is clear that most Americans do not take full advantage of the information on world affairs that is available to them. During presidential election campaigns, and in times of international crisis, a substantial proportion of the population becomes reasonably well informed about some foreign policy issues, but day in and day out it is only a relatively small (although numerically substantial) attentive foreign policy public that regularly follows international developments. And within this attentive public there is an even smaller group, which we have called the active foreign policy public, that regularly makes its voice heard.

The importance of the active foreign policy public is, however, far greater than its numbers. It plays a significant part in ensuring that international affairs do not become the exclusive preserve of special interests or of an official elite. It serves, in effect, as a surrogate for the general public in regard to issues about which few others have become informed. At times, members of the active foreign policy public become opinion leaders and mobilize some of their fellow citizens to support or oppose a candidate or a policy. Foreign policy officials are occasionally chosen from the ranks of this group, as when the President appoints as ambassador or special representative a private citizen who has long taken an interest in international affairs and perhaps has spoken out on issues involving our relations with other countries.

It is the existence of quality mass media providing extensive day-to-day coverage of international affairs, as well as of specialized magazines, journals and books, that makes it possible for these citizens to take an active interest in foreign policy. Without these sources, members of the active foreign policy public would be unable to form opinions and comment intelligently on current developments. The necessary information would be confined to a closed circle of officials and persons with special privileges, as it is in some countries.

But many of these quality media could not survive if their audiences were confined to members of the active foreign policy public. Foreign coverage, as we have seen, is expensive. Viable commercial news organizations must have audiences of substantial size if they are to meet their costs. It is here that the larger *attentive* foreign policy public plays a vital role. Even though most members of this group do not take an active part in trying to shape foreign policies, the fact that they read quality publications and watch serious television programs helps to ensure that these publications and programs survive. Their interest in itself is a positive force. And it is from the attentive foreign policy public that those who take an active part in speaking and writing on foreign affairs are recruited.

Members of the attentive foreign policy public, in turn, are often recruited from the ranks of the public at large, and in this recruiting process the general mass media—not only those that provide extensive foreign affairs coverage—are a significant factor. They provide only a limited range of international news, but this news is available every day. While investigations such as those in Cincinnati and Findlay show that exposure to information about foreign affairs does not automatically lead to greater interest in them, the general media offer a starting point for those few who do wish to develop such an interest. Foreign coverage in the popular news sources can lead individuals to consult more specialized media. It is of particular importance in educational programs, which often use the evening television news or articles in the daily newspaper to introduce students to world affairs. Stories about international developments in the general media provide a constant reminder that membership in the attentive and active foreign policy publics is open to any who are willing and able to do their homework.

Of what should this homework consist? On the basis of discussions in the foregoing chapters we can offer a few suggestions. First of all, it involves adoption of a critical approach to international news: keeping in mind that the American definition of news is not necessarily the same as that in other countries; taking into account the problems that confront foreign correspondents; weighing the reliability of the sources to which news reports attribute particular bits of information; making allowances for what may have been omitted due to pressures of space and time on harried editors.

Second, those who wish to deepen their understanding of world affairs are well advised to consult several media and not to rely on any single one. Television can offer unique perspectives; newspapers often provide greater detail; magazines frequently contain more comprehensive treatments of developments that extend over a period of time. As far as those interested in the international scene are concerned, the various mass media complement each other much more than they compete.

Third, advantage should be taken of supplementary sources other than the news media, for they provide much valuable background and new insights on contemporary world events. These sources are available in nearly all communities. They may consist of books and specialized journals in the library or courses at a nearby university. They may be foreign students, other visitors from abroad, or recently returned travelers. The supplementary sources often make some items on the evening news broadcast or in the daily newspaper more meaningful.

Better Media—Or Better Use?

Critics frequently attribute at least part of the blame for difficulties encountered by the United States in its foreign relations to inadequate performance by the news media. Why were we not informed about the extent of Iranian dissatisfaction with the shah? Why didn't foreign correspondents provide more adequate warning that our supplies of oil could be endangered by the action of Arab exporters? Why weren't we told that Fidel Castro would turn Cuba into a Soviet outpost?

Some such negative assessments of media performance may be justified; some not. In some cases we *were* told, but few paid attention.

Certainly, everyone would agree—and most of all journalists—that improved and expanded international reporting is desirable. But, as citizens interested in foreign policy, we should be equally concerned with making better use of the information with which we are already being provided. With all their limitations and problems, the news media are a rich resource that is rarely utilized to the full.

Talking It Over

A Note for Students and Discussion Groups

This pamphlet, like its predecessors in the HEADLINE Series, is published for every serious reader, specialized or not, who takes an interest in the subject. Many of our readers will be in classrooms, seminars or community discussion groups. Particularly with them in mind, we present below some discussion questions—suggested as a starting point only—and references for further reading.

Discussion Questions

As the authors point out, one idea behind news coverage of world events is that the people must be well informed if they are to play their proper role in shaping foreign policy decisions. What is that proper role, in your view?

Since the first newspapers were established centuries ago, the nature of the reading public has changed—and corresponding changes have taken place in the news content of the papers. What developments account for these changes? In general, do you think the changes are for the better or not? Explain your view.

In Communist countries as well as in many developing countries, the official view of the function of the news media is, as the authors put it, "not to inform but to assist"—a view in sharp contrast with the free-press traditions of the industrial West. If you had to uphold both sides in a debate between these two views, what arguments would you stress on each side?

Chapter 3 describes some of the ways in which correspondents for U.S. news media abroad do their work, and the conditions they face in different countries. Of the correspondents you have seen on TV news, or whose bylines you recognize in the newspapers, which do you consider do the best reporting job? What makes their work better than average?

The authors point out that only a few major newspapers in the United States print enough foreign news and analysis to meet the needs of the small but influential "active" foreign policy public. On the other hand, editors and publishers generally claim to devote a larger share of the space in their papers to foreign news than the *average* reader's interests would justify. In view of this broad picture, would you say newspapers in this country provide enough foreign news or not?

In view of the evidence that people often form an opinion on a complex problem on the strength of very little knowledge, what weight do you think policy-makers in a democracy should give to the results of national opinion polls on complex issues of foreign policy?

How do you account for the fact (see Chapter 6) that, in several "saturation" public information campaigns on international subjects, most of the people who showed increased attention to the subject were those who were already interested? Does this mean that such campaigns are not valuable? Explain your view.

In their concluding chapter the authors explain how, in their view, the "quality" mass media and the "general" mass media both play an important part in the foreign policy process. Do you agree with their analysis or not? Why?

READING REFERENCES

Almond, Gabriel, *The American People and Foreign Policy*, 2nd ed. Westport, Ct., Greenwood, 1977.

Batscha, Robert M., *Foreign Affairs News and the Broadcast Journalist*. New York, Praeger, 1973.

Cohen, Bernard C., *The Press and Foreign Policy*. Princeton, Princeton University Press, 1963 (paper).

Davison, W. Phillips, Boylan, James, and Yu, Frederick T.C., *Mass Media: Systems and Effects*. New York, Praeger, 1976.

Desmond, Robert W., *The Information Process: World News Reporting to the Twentieth Century.* Iowa City, University of Iowa Press, 1978.
Gans, Herbert J., *Deciding What's News: A Study of CBS Evening News, NBC Nightly News, Newsweek and Time.* New York, Pantheon, 1979.
Graber, Doris A., *Mass Media and American Politics.* Washington, Congressional Quarterly Press, 1980.
Hohenberg, John, *Foreign Correspondence: The Great Reporters and Their Times.* New York, Columbia University Press, 1967 (paper).
Hopkins, Mark W., *Mass Media in the Soviet Union.* New York, Pegasus, 1970.
Levering, Ralph B., *The Public and American Foreign Policy, 1918-1978.* New York, Morrow, for the Foreign Policy Association, 1978 (paper).
Lippmann, Walter, *Public Opinion.* New York, Free Press, 1965 (paper).
_____, *The Phantom Public.* New York, Harcourt, 1925.
Patterson, Thomas E., *The Mass Media Election.* New York, Praeger, 1980.
Reston, James, *Artillery of the Press.* New York, Harper & Row, 1967.
Righter, Rosemary, *Whose News? Politics, the Press and the Third World.* New York, Times Books, 1978.
Rosenau, James N., *Public Opinion and Foreign Policy.* Philadelphia, Pa., The Philadelphia Book Co., 1961 (paper).
Shanor, Donald R., *Soviet Europe.* New York, Harper & Row, 1975.
Siebert, Frederick S., et al., *Four Theories of the Press: The Authoritarian, Libertarian, Social Responsibility and Soviet Communist Concepts of What the Press Should Be and Do.* Champaign, Ill., University of Illinois Press, 1963 (paper).
Steele, A.T., *The American People and China.* New York, McGraw-Hill, 1966.
Yu, Frederick T.C., *Mass Persuasion in Communist China.* New York, Praeger, 1964.